Colorfast

The Meter is Irregular

Volume 4

Roddy

Colorfast

The Meter is Irregular, Volume 4

Roddy

Copyright © 2015 Rodney Charles

Published by 1st World Publishing
P.O. Box 2211, Fairfield, Iowa 52556
tel: 641-209-5000 • fax: 866-440-5234
web: www.1stworldpublishing.com

First Edition

LCCN: 2014937134

ISBN: 978-1-4218-3751-2

Acknowledgments

The friendly, aromatic coffee houses
of Fairfield, Iowa.

for Nandini

The inside of me is spilling out.

Finally.

Some Memories of You

Seduced by pigment and skill,
Indian grand masters
strewn in haphazard piles covering your tiny pink feet,
a white marble palace,
floating in the mystery of Taj Lake,
rich with the aroma of Udaipur curry and sweet chai,
lying breathless,
midnight in Rajasthan,
the Milky Way made its home in your eyes.

In a photo flash,
we assembled every familiar moment,
our common history,
forever rumored
like desert sand,
crystal upon crystal,
forming mountains and seas.

Do you remember the miles ticking by on dusty roads,
when time stopped for love,
chauffeured in a shiny cream Ambassador
like bleached bowler hats on wheels?
An orthodox Indian rental.

Do you remember craving souls,
ravenous on the side of the road,
first-timers,
beasts in human bodies,
unfamiliar with the Milky Way,
knowing only predation, hunger, and fear?

Words have no value.
Love does all the talking.

Remember
eager Chilean seas refusing the limits of coastal
boulders,
endless Saskatchewan sunsets exposing earthy amber
curves
and stolen kisses frozen in endangered Athabasca
glaciers?

Remember
rocky plateaus,
electric assure skies over Taos,
horses neighing in the darkness,
anticipating the sun,
a prayer too pure for words?

You may have lost your hat to the Rio Gande.
but I'll get it back for you.
All rivers pour into the deep sea eventually.

Remember

the high Andes,
our garbage bag and cardboard family toboggan,
the giddy mountain glee that echoes back to Canada,
and hot cocoa like prehistoric sludge?

Remember

the fear in our four-year-old's voice,
first to reach the pilgrim crucifix.
"Why did they hurt him Honey?"
"Why did they hurt him Honey?"
echoes back two thousand years,
with tears no father has rightly reconciled.

The warm Caribbean Sea still runs in my veins,
the taste of salt on your lips,
waves teasing playfully,
caressing our tan, oiled flesh
like buoyant alchemists
transforming cares to gold.

You knew when you met me,
I would yield my treasure:
stillness, gravity, and sunlight,
friendship, compassion,
and happiness,
white powder beaches, vast ocean waves,
Canadian skies,
and the Milky Way in my eyes.

Poetry, like beach glass,
excites my searching soul,
when new and richer colors wash ashore,
completing our family collection.

Infinity consumes me again.
Brilliance and passion
are less than street dust.
Thoughts are daybreak vapors that pass away
as the sun burns through.

Breathless, the fiery sun
is a tiny flickering thing.
My knees buckle involuntarily,
and my lips kiss the soil
that grew this immeasurable domain—
echoing
from the mighty Redwoods
to the North Pacific Coast,
the Milky Way in our eyes.

The whispering clouds,
asleep in the Grand Canyon,
overflow with children's laughter,
inspiring holy awe,
curing the lonely
and those who fear the attack at midnight.

Its resounding caverns echo the depth of our single soul.
All awe is self-directed
and mountains become pinpricks;
clouds become tears,
cleansing the roaring Colorado,
spilling with joy,
urgently exploding to impregnate the Pacifica.

Remember

street jazz in Amsterdam,
french fries with mayonnaise
decorating your tee-shirt and jeans,
newly-wed jitters
and a 6.2 earthquake that rubbled
cathedrals and rattled our honeymoon lodge?

Did I ever tell you the favor granted us by the
Madonna of La Gleize?

Remember

the pew of Vincent van Gogh?
We gleaned our own genius there, just as he had
hoped,
and paid him with mirthful indebtedness.
We shed tears, hidden in tulips, for little Ann Frank,
who longed for canal buses and passersby,
concealed within the emerald enclosure of her natural
humanity.

Remember

the Michigan flood that bankrupt Chicago?
We owned those city streets,
dodging fire hoses and subway sumps
as we dressed your humility in chic

Remember

high-rise blimps,
overstuffed breasts
that winked at us three times,
from three directions,
exposing the benevolent nature of inner Las Vegas?

Remember

penthouse panoramas of manmade glitter
surrounded by desert powder on the eastern wake of
Death Valley?

Remember

Dakota
where half a ray of twilight struck a patch of Bad-
lands,
opening sensuous eyes to shockwaves
that shuddered like the alchemy of truth,
instructing us that one surrender
is sweeter than a hundred empires?

Dakota mountain goats
and Nepali monks
know surrender,
sunning themselves on the high, northern peaks,
inhaling the setting sun,
inspired by poetry
and the faith that warmth will return when morning
comes.

Encased by love on every side,
our children's bodies bury us like avalanche boulders,
tumbling out of bed,
while half a ray of morning strikes the splintered logs
of Hotel Roughrider—
and grace falls through,
a reminder that essence is wealth.
Mountain goats know surrender.

Remember

cotton fields, poorly cultivated,
baskets brimming with almonds,
same-day fresh, big as robins eggs?

Remember

plump, bumper vine-grapes
dripping down our chins,
ready for Napa's first press?

Remember

tasting ashen smoke,
dense as Newfoundland fog;
choking Jack London Lodge
and smothering our emerald lakeside,
as we joined the urgent race,
north toward Hood Mountain?

Remember

Champaign for breakfast in Fargo?
A just reward for road-weary travelers
and those who fought the Red River flood.
Our eyes shone like secret lovers
who abandoned kingdoms for mud huts,
no longer subject to false judgment,
ardent only for mystic embrace.

Remember

the Milky Way,
stars and planets who see and hear inside our soul,
and repay to us, what we give to them?

Remember

the vacuum of space
that vibrates within the music of Earth
and understands
the meaning of laughter and tears?

Remember

a growing embryo,
endowed with the follies of Plato and Hermione,
a baby girl,
nine months,
and the thrill of constellations
pointing to the throne of Capricorn?

Remember

a growing embryo,
a baby boy,
Libran born, like his father,
with Mars guiding Solomon
and hinges that swing like experimental jazz?

We did not build our home of earth and trees.
We built baby ducks and irresistible intentions—
wisdom and laughter,
offered to the vacuum of space,
its stars and planets,
and the Milky Way in our children's eyes.

We built
a kingdom
with sunlight, azure skies,
lyrics and harmonies,
and five hundred thousand miles of roadway,
which led us to hold
that truth gambles everything for love.

Remember

Nizamuddin AC2?
Ricket and clatter,
bunks and berths,
jolts and squat toilets,
"Gharam chaaaaiiii!,"
Delhi to Hyderabad.
And twenty-four hours of laughter and love
in perfect sync,
with tracks, clacks,
muffs, and moans
from whacked, worn, dusty travelers.

No one doubts love
onboard a speeding bullet—
one direction, one purpose:
Hyderabad.
Excuses are for idle minds
that jitter from lack of deep rest,
holy wine, and endless seas.

No one doubts love
when the ground opens beneath their feet
and all that remains are tears
and sweet cries of liberation—
a deliverance that bathes black coal dust from our face,
leaving us free to inhale sacred air
and embrace the laughter of children.

Awake in love,
nothing left to accomplish,
each act is reverent prayer.

Remember Hyderabad—

where I learned your heritage firsthand
from the playful eyes of Italian marble statues
that gazed across acres of green English gardens
and spoke of manicure, wealth, servants, and family
palaces
in transition from dispossession and loss of class.

The Gymkhana Club
charmed my curious senses.
Images of pint-sized Durgesh,
grass stains and leaves
hidden in a thicket of hair,
and stories imagined
still echoing from British architecture,
white marble floors covered in antique carpets
and stale leather chairs.

Family picnics and dances
are nested within trees beckoning to be climbed.
Stage shows and movies on the lawn,
swinging and singing and lounging near the pool,
catered by a regiment of attendants,
standing alert,
like British penguins
eager to satisfy the least appeal.

I don't know what pulled me to the men's lounge—
expensive cologne,
dry liquor,
pungent tobacco, thick like molasses.
Distressing trophies of fully skinned tiger heads,
racks of forest deer,
wild boar,
and jungle crowns, unrecognizable,
mounted high like cathedral beehive cells,
stretching forty feet to the upmost limit of the ceiling.

Or what pulled me onward to the bridge room and
library—
ancient catacombs
that smacked of decadence
and ten thousand nights of drunken mal-conscience.

This club has secrets to keep—
secrets of loyalties found and lost,
secrets of true love and hidden passions,
secrets of a way of life,
lost,
never to be revived.

Remember

pondering the rubble of your mother's heritage
buried beneath a sea of change?
Then, palatial, a southern lodge,
accented with Rolls-Royce and Chrysler—
now, a high-rise complex
with a hundred forgotten apartments,
ignoring once lush domestic gardens
filled with family stories of snakes and robbers,
blindly overlooking unheeded parking lots,
convenient shops,
arcade glitter,
and flaunted boutiques.

Do you feel the bee sting of monsoon memories?

Remember

we did not build our home of marble and gold.
We built mystic conversation and irresistible inten-
tions,
wisdom, and laughter,
offered to the vacuum of space,
its stars and planets,
and the Milky Way.

We built kingdoms
with sunlight, azure skies,
lyrics and harmonies,
and five hundred thousand miles of roadway,
which led us to see
that truth gambles everything for love.

Awake,
nothing left to achieve,
each breath
is prayer.

Do you remember

South Indian zingers on rout to Jubilee Hills—
spices assaulting our bellies from stem to stern,
beads of sweat from my bald topper to my dripping
chin?

Remember

walking, or skipping, down Lover's Lane,
where massive Sugerloaf boulders fell from the sky,
sixty-six million years ago,
leaving curved trails,
dark corners,
and the mystery of puppy love—
Durgesh and Kamal,

first love, first touch,
and the mark of youth's betrayal,
roughly healed.

Like a buried culture,
the beauty and mystery of Jubilee's formations
suffered the heavy hammers of urban sprawl,
leaving only remembrances—
its majesty
hidden within the industrial dust of its soul
and yours.

At its peak,
a new vista rises—
invoking a new age,
illumined with digits and light speed information.
HITEC City sparkles like a silicon, marble, fairytale
oasis,
summoning images of The Wizard of Oz
and the ice palaces of Hans Christian Anderson.

Like me,
you keep secrets inside yourself,
but I see the tears behind your eyes,
pregnant with sentimentality.

Before us,
a testament to India's cultural leadership—
a contemporary Taj Mahal.
Global digital magnates—
Gates, Jobs, Sysco, Dell—
in search of genius and inexpensive talent.

Breathless for a moment,
we inhale the monumental complex—
a carpet of blue-veined marble thrown haphazard in
the dessert,
blending ancient sculpture, cutting edge geodesics,
and gushing Italian fountains
overflowing into multi-tiered white agate canals.

Brushing your hand,
I am drawn inward for a moment,
where memories consume my vision
of the first time
—our first time.
India airlines;
Delhi to Jaipur.
"Feel my hands, Mr. Charles."

You were cold, like iced fish,
and veiled apprehension sparkled behind your eyes.
Like Arthur's knight, I burnished your bloodless blue
fingertips,
surrendering the warmth of my fearless Canadian
circulation.

I think I knew then.
I think I knew we would look back one day
and remember the Milky Way,
the vacuum of space,
the kingdoms of sunlight and azure skies,
and five hundred thousand miles of roadway,
gambling everything for love.

Remember

hard times—
snares set by our worn-out egos,
desperate for air,
chasing illusions like troll fishers hauling in their
catch,
hoping for a blessed bounty
to dupe off inexorable mortality.

Remember

Bankruptcy,
losing hope,
assurance,
refuge—
losing you,
losing identity,
and the lie that self worth
is valued at 2.2 million dollars.

Remember

integrity—
a rising phoenix,
a pauper daring to dream,
rebuilding a vision,
a digital Alexandria,

1st World Library,
a spiritual quest,
a dozen pilgrim treks to mother India
imploring a singular boon—
all knowledge on every computer.

Remember

audacity—
setting out to find God
and finding ourselves in the dead of night,
awake, alone, breathing love from four corners,
nothing left to accomplish,
each act—a prayer.

Remember

the poetry of footprints?
Parenting Teenage Werewolves,
leaving a trail for them to follow—
"I am healthy, happy, alert, active, fresh, young and
wise."
A nighttime prayer affirmed,
constructed with neuron and synapse
and manifest with laughter, realization,
and the Milky Way
E V E R Y W H E R E.

Remember

forty-four years of fasting—
whispers echoing from organs and tissues,
granting hygiene, self-illumination, and the absence
of fear.
It's proof that "past is past."
Let it go,
forget,
and never regret the audacity of self-ignorance.

Like a mad wolf chasing ghosts in the forest,
we may have suffered greatly,
and misled the lost, by being lost,
but finally,
bathed in the unfading ocean,
we abandon our soiled weary clothes,
and naked,
let the waves crash against us—
your tiny hand in mine,
the Milky Way in our eyes

Together.
Together.

Remember

rarified air
and purple mountain ski lifts in Aspen—
your tiny hand in mine,
higher than the clouds,
wrapped in the Milky Way,
and five layers of insulation.

I gave you my coat at the peak of Snowmass
Mountain,
when your lips turned polar blue.

I know what keeps you warm inside,
but I'll keep your secret.
When the ocean is calling,
love leaves us nowhere to hide.

Listen to the willing waves lapping the sandy shore,
coaxing it to surrender its mysteries.
Pay little attention to blue mountain ice.
Soon it will sacrifice everything
for the warm wine of spring,
its white rivers raging with passion,
eager to press itself hard against the sea.

Remember

spelunking
in Crystal Caverns,
South of St. Louis,
and the winding, water-polished cavities of boyhood
Huckleberry,
Twain's caves in Hannibal,
your tiny hand in mine,
buried beneath a billion tons of stardust and silence?

Remember

listening to the stillness of the Milky Way?
Voices have no meaning here—
just babbling business crushed by four billion years of
rock.
Shhhhh.
That's enough for now.
Listen.
Just listen,
with your tiny hand in mine.

Remember

our rainy-day trek—
hilltop hiking in British Columbia,
Canadian snakes near Osoyoos hiding beneath every
marshy footstep?

I offered no warning.
Had I told you what squeezed below your tiny feet
you would have panicked and died of fright.
I kept quiet.

Snakes are snakes,
but fear imparts demonic power—
venomous bites that halt our heart and breath.

Fear is a serpent that slips into our open mouth in
deep, dark sleep
and lurks inside our bellies
till we puke and choke it out,
like cancer cast out by the light of God.

When I think about the grey hooded snakes
coiled inside the bowels of men,
I'm amazed I can eat at all.

Remember

whitewater rafting in Banff,
our faces shining with sunburned passion?

Glacial waters,
like the fragrance of truth,
holding healing powers,
restore worn-out reveries with new life
and new craving.
Desire is everything for river rapids.

Churning torrents
spitting icy foam,
knife-edged rocks
ogling us with hungry eyes,
eager to consume our yellow flotation.

Mountain waters cannot fake satisfaction.
Imitation, though sweet to the tongue on first blush,
leaves us famished for sustenance
and parched for the rich thrust
of risk and enlightenment.
Desire is everything for river rapids.

Remember

Borglum's granite at Mount Rushmore?
The wonder of artistry
breathes continuous praise
into democratic doctrines.

Keystone's temple buckled our knees,
melting our immigrant status
like a toddler's birthday candle,
quickly extinguished,
to ravish the sweet butter and cake within.

Remember

Rushmore, mute—
inspired by the roaring prayers
of a million Harley Davidson's,
rumbling one hundred miles
from Sturgis,
its epicenter,
to the vacuums of space?

Remember

Our senses transfixed,
reverberating,
in multiple aftershocks,
echoing through the canyons
of Badlands National Park,

crumbling false resistance
to America's wakening soul
and our US citizenship?

We are again bewitched
by the almighty flame of Liberty
and the deafening thunder
of Harley mantras:
There is no easy walk to freedom,
faltering, we destroy ourselves.

Remember

our family mammoth—
a massive Hummer, canary yellow,
and two thousand weary, weathered roadways to
Katrina?

New Orleans received us like long lost clan folk at a
family funeral.
New Orleans knows what it means to gamble the
Milky Way.
New Orleans knows the breach of truth,
its stars and planets, the vacuum of space, and the
music of Earth.
New Orleans knows that mercy will enter through
any open doorway,
gambling everything for love.

Remember

Niagara—
four pilgrims bundled in plastic ponchos
elevated by oblations,
thundering ten feet
from the Maid of the Mist,
a vessel designed to carry souls to the font of God,
where precious wine is human merriment
and death?
God's grand illusion,
is tested by torrents of pouring opportunities.

Those faithful will die of laughter,
while those afraid,
live as hypocrites,
blaming the wicked world,
insulting the omnipotence that recycles
every drop of mighty Niagara,
who roars,
"The wine God loves
is human honesty."

Remember

Christmas mornings—
discovering carrot crumbs left behind by hungry
reindeer,
half-eaten cookies from hasty Santa,
Irish carols bright and merry as Christmas wrapping,
and burstable anticipation?

Remember

children's eyes glazed and eager,
itching to unwrap their smiles,
and Jesus,
with his guardians,
topping our recycled pine,
looking down from the right hand of God,
the Milky Way in his eyes?

Time stops,
suspended again,
with memories of Mary's womb—
dense love, consuming and impenetrable like Rajast-
hani fog.

We share uncommon joy,
like four candles burning together into one flame.
There is no future time or place,
nowhere else to be in this worldly venture,
just here,

in this singular familiarity—
home,
awake,
nothing left to realize.
Each breath—the prayers of children,
bounding in the safety of Super Mario,
and the guardians of God, looking down,
atop our synthetic Christmas pine,
bathed in the Milky Way,
its starlight blushing in our eyes.

This magic—
time
and its illusion.

Remember

cuddling sickly sweet wine,
tipsy, in a secluded corner of
Coralville's Olive Garden?
Our 23rd wedding anniversary—
I emptied the well.

I lassoed the moon,
captured the Milky Way,
the music of Earth,
and five hundred thousand miles of roadway,
gambling everything for new courage,
with warm words
that return to us,
what we give to them.

Remember

the journey was lonely for a while.
A hunger for transparency—
inner revelations,
secrets,
impossible to explain.

Had I told you the truth,
the enigmas of my soul,
mysteries evolving like creation,
you would have trembled with fear.

You did not see my crucifixion,
inner ecstasy and outer insanity.
You were not there
when language immerged from creation
and angels found infant wings.

You did not see the Milky Way inhaled,
its stars and planets inside my soul,
a limitless stream of cool blue liquid space,
a black hole at the center of everything,
consumed by nature's oceanic mouthpiece,
never ending, never ending, never ending.

But I feel you
asleep at night,
a wakeful witness to extraordinary dreams,
and shed a tear,
aware that dreams are lifelike,
and like life,
sometimes leave us aching and yearning
for the crystal waters of being—
the ones that draw us five hundred thousand miles,
drinking deeply
from the Milky Way,
with nowhere to hide.

Silent, awake at night,
I hear your chirping,
your hidden sacrifices
and unwilling admittances,
swimming alone,
unable to find shore.

I cannot describe
the ocean of your dreams,
but one day, I'll take you there,
and we'll be forgiven for forgetting,
that what we really want
is to gamble everything for another moment.

Together.

Together
again.

About the Author

August Iowa
Twilight crickets rev their engines
Racing to mate
Expecting a hit

Like desert fathers
Muttering mantras for centuries
I feel the rhythm of your rubbing
In step with my snoring remains

Just another trance
Like children searching
For sex and war
Worth only dream gold

Don't be satisfied
With the gist of poetry
Discern the breathing
Of the artist

Other Books by Rodney Charles

The Meter is Irregular
Volume 1
Parenting Teenage Werewolves

The Meter is Irregular
Volume 2
Unleashing Teenage Werewolves

The Meter is Irregular
Volume 3
Inner Life of Turtles